Farm
MACHINES

First published 1987 by J.M. Dent & Sons Ltd

Picturemac edition published 1990 by
Pan Macmillan Children's Books
A division of Pan Macmillan Limited
London and Basingstoke
Associated companies throughout the world

Reprinted 1990 (twice), 1991, 1992

ISBN 0-333-51445-9

A CIP catalogue record for this book is available from the British Library

Printed in Hong Kong

The author would like to thank the many people who have
helped with this book, with special thanks to:
Lesley Bowes; Elspeth Clark; Farmers Weekly; The Hildred
Partnership, Goring-on-Thames; David Taylor,
Farm Manager, Preshaw Estate, Southampton; Alan
Williams, Farm Manager, Copas Bros., Cookham

For Lucy and Peter

Farm
MACHINES

Jane Miller

M

MACMILLAN CHILDREN'S BOOKS

Tractors are used in
most kinds of farm work.

They can be driven on rough
and muddy ground.

The blue tractor on the *left* page and the green one *above*
are both pulling ploughs.

The tractor on the *left* has just come back from carting straw
for the pigs' bedding.

Tractors also pull other machinery like
seed drills and balers.

Here are some big tractors
used in Australia to pull
ploughs.

The plough on the *left*
is 14.5 metres wide.

The one *below* is called a
'stump jump' plough
because it can jump over
roots and bumps.

In England, smaller ploughs
such as these
are called cultivators.

After the fields have been ploughed it is time to sow the seed.

The seed drill *above* is sowing seed in autumn that will be ripe for harvesting the following summer.

You can see the farmer on the *left* loading a combine drill that sows seed and fertilizer together. The harrow behind it spreads earth over the seeds.

In spring the farmer drives the tractor over
the young crops, spreading fertilizers
from spreaders such as these.

Some of the plants are flattened
by the tractor's tyres,
but they quickly stand up again.

Crops must be given fertilizers because the
soil does not contain all the nourishment that
the plants need to make them grow.

See how the boom of the crop sprayer on the *right* unfolds like two wings. It is 24 metres long from tip to tip.

In the picture *below* it sprays fungicide on the wheat crop to kill any blight while it is growing.

In the picture *above* the farmer takes
a bowser full of water to the fields
with which to mix the sprays.

On the *left* the potato crop
is being sprayed with fungicide to destroy
blight and aphids.

When the grass has grown in spring
the farmer mows it to make silage which
will be food for cattle in winter.

In the picture *below left* a machine called
a forage harvester picks it up,
and chops and blows it into the trailer
which takes it to the farm.

Below, a red fork-lift truck is being
used to lift the grass into the building
which is called a silage clamp, where
the silage is made.

On the *left* is a tree-digging machine that digs up the roots, wraps them for protection and takes the tree to be planted somewhere else.

Having brought a sheep to the yard in the transport box, the shepherd gives his dogs a ride in it.

Above: after the grass is cut for hay,
a hay turner tosses and spreads it.

Above: a pick-up baler scoops it up
and makes it into oblong bales.

Below: the fork-lift truck loads them on the trailer,
eight bales at a time. Hay is used to feed animals.

Below: a big green baler rolls
the hay into huge round bales.

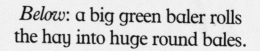

In summer the crops are ripe for harvesting. The farmer has driven the combine harvester to the fields. He has towed parts of it on the trailer.

The picture on the *right* shows him putting the combine harvester together.

Now it is ready to go. It will cut and thresh the crops, separating the grain from the straw.

Right: another combine harvester is cutting and threshing a field of wheat. You can see the grain pouring down the spout into the grain trailer which takes it to the farm.

Sometimes two combine harvesters work together so as to finish the field more quickly in case it rains.

The farmers on top of this
red combine harvester are
watching the grain pouring out.

The baler *above*, and the green
one on the *opposite* page are tying
and dropping round bales of straw.

The fork-lift truck takes the
bales to the farm.

A pick-up baler *above* is making oblong bales.
At the back you can see the bale sledge
that collects and leaves them in sets of eight.

The straw will be used for animal bedding.

Left: on this farm in Wales a lorry
is used to take the bales to the barn.

Some farms use a bale wagon to gather the oblong bales. It stacks them inside. This one on the *left* can carry 104 of them.

Right: the machine on the front of the blue tractor is called a bale loader. It picks up the bales in the sets of eight that have been left by the bale sledge, and puts them on to the trailer.

Here on the *left* the farmer is towing a load of bales back to the barn.

The smaller blue tractor is using a machine called a back loader to pour pig food into the tote bins on the trailer.

The red tractor is working a front loader. Look at the farmer unloading the pig food into the blue bin.

When the farmer needs to move his pigs to another part of the farm, he catches them and transports them in the pig trailer.

Water troughs sometimes freeze in winter, so the farmer has to take out a water-cart to give the pigs a drink.

Cutting the hedge with a hedge flail

Milking time

Firewood for the winter

This digger (called a JCB) is making the ground level for a new farm building.

Autumn is the season to harvest potatoes. See the pickers collecting them in sacks as they drop off the green machine called an elevator digger.

Big potato harvesters like this are used on large farms.

The harvester on the *left* is working along the rows of potatoes, digging them up and dropping them off the elevator into the trailer.

The machine on the *right*, called a grader, cleans the potatoes and sorts them by size. Big ones go on a conveyor to the store behind. Small ones are separated for animal food.

Huge harvesters like the one on the *right* lift the sugar beet from the fields in the autumn.

Below: the green machine called a cleaner-loader shakes off the dirt and stones from the beet. Then it loads the beet on to the lorry which takes it to the factory to be used for making sugar which we eat.

These are only some of the marvellous kinds of machinery now being used on farms.

Also by Jane Miller

Farm Alphabet Book
Farm Counting Book
Farm Noises
Farm Seasons

For a complete list of Picturemac titles write to

Pan Macmillan Children's Books
18–21 Cavaye Place, London SW10 9PG